Kama Sutra

The History About Kama Sutra And Ancient Love Making Techniques

By: More Sex More Fun Book Club

Table of Contents

Introduction

For many people when they hear the term Kama Sutra, they immediately think of a borderline pornographic book full of illicit sex positions that only people who are incredibly flexible would ever try. However, this is not all that the Kama Sutra is. In reality, the Kama Sutra presents itself as a guide on how to live a virtuous and gracious life with emphasis on the nature of love, family life and other aspects of the pleasure oriented aspects of the human life. Ultimately, only twenty percent of the Kama Sutra is about sexual positions.

The Kama Sutra is one of three ancient texts that were written in the Sanskrt language to describe the goals of life. Written by a north Indian scholar by the name of Vatsyayna Mallanaga, the Kama Sutra was written in the second century CE and literally means the Treatise on Pleasure. The majority of the book is about philosophy and the theory of love. It covers what triggers love, what sustains love and when it is good or bad.

This book is aimed to guide you through the ancient text of the Kama Sutra and show you how you can use its teachings to bring passion and happiness into your relationships. We are also going to cover briefly on some of the sex positions of the kama sutra, and how they can bring more intimacy into your relationships.

Chapter 1: Kama Sutra – A Brief Look At What It Is And Where It Came From

The Kama Sutra documents the sociology of sex as it was in India many centuries ago. It is a famous book that has been translated many times over. Many people consider the Kama Sutra to be unoriginal and believe that the author, Vatsyana Mallanaga most likely was a reworking of the manuals that already existed in order to write his work. Even so, the Kama Sutra is brings attention to what sexual relationships mean between two people, while still recognizing that that some things are forbidden.

The Kama Sutra encompassed there are sixty-four arts and they were meant to be used by the upper society The text provides detailed descriptions of the rules that both men and women were expected to follow. The rules governed sensuous physical relationships as well as the love and marriage of the couple according to the Hindu law.

While the overall essence of the text relates to being sensuous, the Kama Sutra also ascribes to the traditions and religion of the Hindu society. The primary teaching of the Kama Sutra was that marriages are meant to be happy. Both men and women were to be well versed in the arts of both physical and mental pleasure. The philosophy of the Kama Sutra follows achievements in Dharma, which is religion; Art, which is wealth; Kama, which is pleasures;

and Moksha which is salvation. These are the basic goals that govern life.

The Kama Sutra teaches that all aspects of life are of equal importance and that no aspect should take priority over any other. In order to attain a meaningful life, it is imperative that balance is achieved. If you are able to achieve this balance, you are considered to be living the good life. The Kama Sutra explains that sexuality and erotica are important to human existence and are considered the same as eating. While eating keeps the body alive, sexuality help mankind to propagate.

There are many different stories in ancient Indian scripture that tell about how the Kama Sutra was originated. Below are a couple of examples.

One of the stories that can be found tells that the diety Prjapati, who was the God of Creation, initially declared the ten thousand chapters of the Kama Sutra. The chapters were then assembled by Lord Shiva. Following this, they were further condensed into a great number of chapters. named Shvetaketu. In this story, the role of Vatsyayana was to transcribe the Kama Sutra in Sanskrit.

Another story tells that the Kama Sutra was bestowed on the world by the Indian God Shiva's doorkeeper, Nandi. Nandi, who was a sacred bull, overheard Nandi and his wife, Parvati, while they were making love. Nandi was so inspired that he made an utterance, which was later passed down to humans.

Regardless of where it originated, the Kama Sutra is a book about finding the right partner, maintaining power in a marriage and the art of living. What is unique about the Kama Sutra is that, contrary to popular belief, it does not see women as being erotic subjects, and instead sees them as sexual beings who possess emotions and feelings, which a man should understand in order to achieve the full enjoyment of erotic pleasure.

The Kama Sutra is considered to be the original study of sexuality and quickly became the main resource of subsequent compilations, including the Ananga-Ranga, which is a fifteenth century revised version of the Kama Sutra. However, since it was written in a complex style of Sanskrit it failed to reach readers and fell into obscurity until the late nineteenth century.

One interesting fact about the Kama Sutra is that is actually teaches that the man in a relationship should not sexually approach a woman for the first three nights of the marriage. Instead, he should use this time to understand her feelings, earn her trust and arouse her love. Vatsyayana took a huge leap in the history of Indian sexuality by introducing the idea of love in sex.

In the late nineteenth century, the Kama Sutra began to again gain prominence in India. This occured after a noted linguist and Arabic translator, Sir Richard Burten began working with both Indian and British collaborators to produce an English translation of the Anaga-Ranga. In the translation, Burton made many references to Vatsyayana which led back to the Kama Sutra, and eventually an

English translation of the Kama Sutra was produced as well.

Due to the nature of the content, the Kama Sutra was not legally published in England or the United States until 1962. From the time it was first published in 1883, until it was legally published in 1962, the Kama Sutra gained status as one of the most pirated books in the English language.

Sir Richard Burton's version of the Kama Sutra is the is one of the most well known versions. Not just in the United States but also in India and Europe. Many Hindi and other Indian translations come from Burton's English translation instead of the original Sanskrit source. However, because of this, the true essence of the Kama Sutra has been lost. Where the original Kama Sutra emphasized the importance of the female and her role in the act of lovemaking, Burton's version silences the woman.

The Kama Sutra contains sixty-four arts of love which are made up of acts of love and sexual congress divided into eight methods. The Kama Sutra also explores the pleasures of the woman, as well as heterosexuality, and homosexuality. A few of the other topics the book covers include how to attract a spouse, how to be a good wife and how to strengthen the bonds between people to avoid the need to seek out a different domestic situation.

One of the most basic tenents for Kama Sutra is so there is marriage in relationships so both parties are happy both physically and cerebrally. Some of the topics that Kama Sutra explores are the social concepts for sexual union, getting a wife and about wives and other men. You will also learn about how to attract others to you. In the end, you will learn how to win over someone of the opposite sex. If someone has rejected you, you will learn about that as well.

There are some who believe that you can use the Kama Sutra as a manual for your marriage. While this would be awesome, the Kama Sutra is nowhere near good advice for a monogamous relationship. As you go about reading the Kama Sutra, you are going to realize that the main figure is the courtesan who is the master of various ways in how a woman can please her man.

Something unique about the Kama Sutra is that it pays special attention to the creation of pleasure on the woman. Any man who cannot bring about these pleasures is going to be liable to meet recourse from a woman as they go seek pleasure somewhere else.

The Karma Sutra was one of the original studies for sexuality and therefore became the beginning for any other compilations that came after it. One of those compilations was the Ananga Ranga which built upon the basic tenets for what Vatsyayana believed in. Still, the Kama Sutra is one of the most sought after books even thought it is written in Sanskrit.

It was not until the nineteeth century that the Kama Sutra was picked back up and continued from the traditions that were found in India. Around 1870, Sir Richard Burton worked on translating the Ananga Ranga in which they found many references to Vatsyayana. Due to this, he produced an English version of the Kama Sutra and found that it held a lot of proliferations to the translastions and many versions that can be found based on the original text.

Ananga Ranga

This version is from the fifteenth century and is just an updated version of the Kama Sutra. But, it is more easily accessed than the original version of the Kama Sutra. Because of this, it actually bypassed the Kama Sutra for a long time. The Ananga Ranga was commissioned by a nobleman. Surprisingly, the Ananga Ranga was written by a Hindu poet that used the Kama Sutra as inspiration. You can find the Ananga Ranga in Urdu, Arabic, and even Persian.

When you look at the dedication to the Ananga Ranga you will realize that it has a bit of advice for married couples and how they are supposed to work together in social and sexual settings. In this description, it goes on to describe a female body and talks about the different places on a woman's body and how they are supposed to be pleased. Not only that, but you will find how a male and female are supposed to work together in order to increase their pleasure.

Chapter 2: The Sixty-Four Arts Of The Kama Sutra

Now that we have a general idea of where the Kama Sutra came from as well as what the Kama Sutra truly is, we are going to look a little deeper into the writing to learn what the Kama Sutra teaches. We are going to start with the sixty-four arts of the Kama Sutra.

Vatsyayana listed out sixty-four arts that were make it to where a person appeared more attractive.. These suggestions do not apply to just one gender, which is interesting since many ancient texts tell about the woman making herself attractive for a man, leaving the impression that a man didn't need to do anything to become more attractive for a female.

In the Kama Sutra, Vatsyayana states:

"A public woman, endowed with a good disposition, beauty and other winning qualities, and also versed in the above arts, obtains the name of a Ganika, or public woman of high quality, and receives a seat of honour in an assemblage of men.She is, moreover, always respected by the king, and praised by learned men, and her favour being sought for by all, she becomes an object of universal regard. The daughter of a king too as well as the daughter of a minister, being learned in the above arts, can make their husbands favorable to them, even though these may have thousands of other wives besides themselves.If a wife becomes separated from her husband, and falls into

distress, she can support herself easily, even in a foreign country, by means of her knowledge of these arts. Even the bare knowledge of them gives attractiveness to a woman, though the practice of them may be only possible or otherwise according to the circumstances of each case. A man who is versed in these arts, who is loquacious and acquainted with the arts of gallantry, gains very soon the hearts of women, even though he is only acquainted with them for a short time."

Here is a list of the 64 arts; they are going to be listed in Sanskrit as well as English.

1. Geet Vidya – Art of singing

2. Vadya vidya – Art of playing on musical instruments

3. Nritya vidya – Art of dancing

4. Natya vidya – Art of theatricals

5. Alekhya vidya – Art of painting

6. Viseshakacchedya vidya- Art of paining the face and body with color

7. Tandula-kusuma-bali-vikara – Art of preparing offerings from rice and flowers

8. Pushpastarana – Art of making a covering of flowers for a bed

9. Dasana-vasananga-raga – Art of applying preparations for cleansing teeth cloths and painting the body

10. Mani-bhumika-karma – Art of making the groundwork of jewels

11. Aayya-racana- Art of covering the bed

12. Udaka-vadya – Art of playing music on water

13. Udaka-ghata – Art of splashing with water

14. Citra-yoga – Are of practically applying an admixture of colors

15. Malya-grathana-vikalpa – Art of designing a preparation of wreaths

16. Sekharapida-yojana – Art of practically setting the coronet on the head

17. Nepathya-yoga – Art of practically dressing in the tiring room

18. Karnapatra-bhanga – Art of decorating the tragus of the ear

19. Sugandha-yukti – Art of practical application of aromatics

20. Bhushana-yojana – Art of applying or setting ornaments

21. Aindra-jala – Art of juggling

21. Kaucumara – A kind of art

23. Hasta-laghava – Art of sleight of hand

24. Citra-sakapupa-bhakshya-vikara-kriya – Art of preparing varieties of delicious food

25. Panaka-rasa-ragasava-yojana – Art of practically preparing palatable drinks and tinging draughts with red color.

26. Suci-vaya-karma – Art of needlework and weaving

27. Sutra-krida – Art of playing with thread

28. Vina-damuraka-vadya – Art of playing on the lute and small drum

29. Prahelika – Art of making and solving riddles

30. Durvacaka-yoga – Art of practicing language difficult to be answered by others

31. Pustaka-vacana – Art of reciting books

32. Natikakhyayika-darsana – Art of enacting short plays and anecdotes

33. Kavya-samasya-purana – Art of solving enigmatic verses

34. Pattika-vetra-bana-vikalpa – Art of design and preparation of shield, cane and arrows

35. Tarku-karma – Art of spinning by spindle

36. Takshana – Art of carpentry

37. Vastu-vidya – Art of engineering

38. Raupya-ratna-pariksha – Art of testing silver and jewels

39. Dhatu-vada – Art of metallurgy

40. Mani-raga jnana – Art of tinging jewels

41. Akara jnana – Art of mineralogy

42. Vrikshayur-veda-yoga – Art of practicing medicine or medical treatment by herbs

43. Mesha-kukkuta-lavaka-yuddha-vidhi – Art of knowing the mode of fighting lambs, cocks and birds

44. Suka-sarika-pralapana – Art of maintaining or knowing conversation between male and female cockatoos

45. Utsadana – Art of healing or cleaning a person with perfumes

46. Kesa-marjana-kausala – Art of combing hair

47. Akshara-mushtika-kathana – Art of talking with fingers

48. Dharana-matrika – Art of the use of amulets

49. Desa-bhasha-jnana – Art of knowing provincial dialects

50. Nirmiti-jnana – Art of knowing prediction by heavenly voice

51. Yantra-martika – Art of mechanics

52. Mlecchita-kutarka-vikalpa – Art of fabricating barbarous or foreign sophistry

53. Samvacya – Art of conversation

54. Manasi kavya-kriya – Art of composing verse

55. Kriya-vikalpa – Art of designing a literary work or a medical remedy

56. Chalitka-yoga – Art of practicing as a builder of shrines
57. Abhidhana-kosha-cchando-jnana – Art of the use of lexicography and meters

58. Vastra-gopana – Art of concealment of cloths

59. Dyuta-visesha – Art of knowing specific gambling

60. Akarsha-krida – Art of playing with dice or magnet

61. Balaka-kridanaka – Art of using children's toys

62. Vainayiki vidya – Art of enforcing discipline

63. Vaijayiki vidya – Art of gaining victory

64. Vaitaliki vidya – Art of awakening master with music
    at dawn

You can see that a lot of these arts would have no place in making you more attractive in today's society, however there are some that are still applicable today.

The purpose behind these arts is not to make a good spouse, instead it is to try and make a person who is going to possess the qualities that some wants in a spouse along with making that person feel good about themselves. Indians in the ancient world paid special attention to the details before they could enjoy intercourse Knowledge of the sixty-four arts was important to ensure that the act of foreplay was carried out correctly. We are going to cover foreplay later on in this book, first we are going to cover how the Kama Sutra can bring happiness and health to your body and your mind.

Chapter 3: Kama Sutra – Bringing Happiness And Health To Your Body And Mind

When it is well practiced, the Kama Sutra is able to bring many health benefits to our physical, physiological and mental well being. There are different reasons behind this, some of which include the yoga basis to the sexual positions, tantric massage, as well as encouraging closer relationships between couples.

There are many benefits to the yoga positioning in the lovemaking aspect to the Kama Sutra. Yoga is well known to provide many benefits from flexibility and relaxation to increased blood flow and mental clarity.

Tantric massage is an erotic massage that encourages partners to really get to know one anothers bodies. By becoming familiar with each other's bodies, partners are able to learn what their partner finds arousing outside of the typical arousal spots.

The encouragement of healthy relationships between partners occurs both in and out of the bedroom. The Kama Sutra recognizes that there is a connection between the intimate parts of a relationship as well as the everyday motions a couple goes through. Being able to connect in and outside of the bedroom helps a couple to establish a nurturing bond that cannot be broken.

There are many other ways that a healthy sex life, as laid out in the Kama Sutra, can contribute to your health and happiness.

When they are done correctly, the Kama Sutra positions are designed to encourage bonding and curiousity between partners. Some of the more advanced positions also foster trust in one another in order to balance and not be hurt. Learning how to pleasure one another is a journey that is exciting and invigorating and allows for new feelings to emerge in the relationship.

Sex also aids in the production of hormones such as oxytocin, which keeps you healthy and glowing. Engaging in one hour of sexual activity is equivalent to fifteen minutes of jogging, and can burn up to two hundred calories per session. Sex is thought to fight stress, increase heart health and those who engage in regular sex are said to be less impacted by arthritis, depression, anxiety, and stress.

This isn't to say that you can go and have sex with anyone in order to reap the benefits of having sex. The Kama Sutra promoted having intimate sex with one partner. In order to have intimate sex, there needs to be a connection on a level deeper than simply physical. There needs to be a mental, emotional and spiritual connection between two partners in order to really get any of the benefits of having sex in the way the Kama Sutra lays out.

Today there are many people who feel as though their sex life has fallen into a rut. The act of making love becomes boring and tedious and couples tend to get lost in the day to day routine of their lives. This was true back in the ancient Indian times as well as today. This was why the Kama Sutra spent a lot of time discussing foreplay.

When a relationship fails to have a healthy sex life, the couple often finds that they will eventually have problems in other aspects of their relationship. The act of making love creates a closeness between a man and woman, and this is what the Kama Sutra was created to cultivate.

The Kama Sutra puts a lot of emphasis on foreplay over the actual act of intercourse. In the Kama Sutra's teachings it is emphasized that foreplay should be taken slowly for many reasons. Some of these reasons include:

- Foreplay makes things hotter in the bedroom and builds the anticipation;

- Foreplay allows the man and woman to get to know one another's bodies;

- Foreplay ensures that both partners are peaking with excitement; and

- Foreplay creates a connection between the two partners.

Many people don't truly understand what foreplay is. In today's society we think that foreplay is simply what we do in the moments leading up to sex, and in many cases people feel as though this is unnecessary. The Kama Sutra, however, recognized that intercourse without foreplay can actually be detrimental to the intimacy that two lovers should feel. The Kama Sutra teaches that great love making begins in the mind and preparing for making love is the most important part of the equation.

In the next couple chapters of this book we are going to analyze what foreplay was intended to be, according to the Kama Sutra, and how you can use that information in your personal life.

Chapter 4: Getting Started With Foreplay And The Kama Sutra

When foreplay was written out in the Kama Sutra, there was reference to the servants and other people who would be in the room to help the man set up the room as well as being the woman to him. In today's society, many of us don't have servants that we can rely on to do these things for us. For that reason, the steps to foreplay have been modified from the way it was written to apply to the Indian culture and times it was written for. Instead they have been written as they would be to apply to the lives of the people who are reading this book to learn how to bring more happiness into their lives and relationships. The steps below may seem like a lot of work to get everything ready, but the preparations are sure to increase the excitement and pleasure you and your partner feel making it worth the effort.

1. The first, and most important thing, that needs to be done before you are intimate with your partner is to take the time to relax. After a long, exhausting day at work, you need to take the time to relax both your body and your mind. This relaxation can be achieved in whatever way you find to be the most effective. This can be a hot shower, a nap, or a run. By taking the time to relax before becoming intimate with your partner you are ensuring that you aren't going to be distracted thinking about your day while you are with your partner.

2. The Kama Sutra refers to the room that you and your partner are going to be intimate in as the pleasure room. The decoration of the pleasure room is an important aspect to ensure that both partners are able to be adequately aroused. While we aren't likely to place garlands and bunches of flowers around the room, you can burn some aromatic candles or incense. Some of the scents you could choose to burn include jasmine, cinnamon, or ylang-ylang. Another way to set the mood in the room is to have tantric music playing in the background. The temperature of the room is very important. You want the temperature to be warm, but not too warm. While you want the room to be comfortable, you don't want it to be so comfortable that you are going to curl up and fall asleep. Keep in mind that you are going to want to eliminate all distractions, including TV's, phones, laptops, beepers, and the doorbell.

3. In the Kama Sutra it is stated that upon entering the pleasure room both partners should be freshly cleansed. The purpose of ensure that you are clean is to make sure that your body is appealing to your partner. This is something that hasn't changed with time. This is also a great opportunity to cleanse your day away and start fresh with your partner.

Wear a perfume that is going to arouse your partners senses. It is important to choose a scent that your partner likes over one that you like. If you are unsure what scents your partner likes, it is advised that you use a neutral scent, or no scent at all. Another suggestion is to wear something that is going to be visually appealing to your partner. This doesn't mean that you need to wear something that is revealing, or even buy something new to wear. You can wear a color that your partner likes, or even an outfit that your partner often compliments.

4. The Kama Sutra strongly encourages that you embrace your partner before making love, however it isn't referring to your everyday hug. When you are embracing according to the Kama Sutra instructions, you are using much more than your arms. You will be touching, rubbing, and pressing with the front part of your body. The Kama Sutra says that you should avoid using your hands to caress, and instead enjoy the touching sensation from one another's bodies. This can be done before you enter your pleasure room, as well as when you are deep into the act of foreplay.

5. Make the bed with clean sheets and pillow cases. Place one pillow on each end of the bed. Next to the bed you should have a couch and a low table or stool that you can place your massage oils as well as any other items you may choose to use.

6. The Kama Sutra encourages you to share a light meal together, Avoid heavy foods, as these are more likely to make you feel uncomfortable and sleepy after you are done eating. Instead you can feed one another small bites of fruits and other aphrodisiac foods. In the original script of the Kama Sutra, Vatsyayana stated that the man would play with the ties that was holding the womans clothing on. This can be easily modified for modern times, with the man running his fingertips along the back of the neckline of the woman's shirt, or if she is

wearing a skirt along the hem of the skirt where her leg begins to show.

7. While you are eating, have a romantic conversations. At this time you should be focused on showing your partner how much you love, trust and care about them. Bring up any past romantic getaways and erotic imagery. Use your words to get their imaginations wild with anticipation. Vatsyayana said that at this time the man would take the woman out onto the balcony and show her the moon and the stars. He would point out the constellations and the conversation would slowly shift from neutral topics with a vague sexual subtext, to more obvious erotic imagery.

Now that you have an idea on how foreplay begins, we are going to take a look at what aphrodisiac foods are and then explore the embraces and kisses that the Kama Sutra outlines as being appropriate for foreplay.

Chapter 5: Aphrodisiac Foods

An aphrodisiac is something that stimulates sexual desire. There are some foods that are believe to stimulate pleasure centers and increase the sex drive and desire of the people eating them. There are different aphrodisiacs in every culture. In the in Kama Sutra, the aphrodisiac foods that were recommended included rice mixed with wild honey as well as a mix of ground up pumpkin seeds, almonds, sugar cane the root of the bamboo that were mixed into milk and honey.

The combinations above may seem a little weird to people today. Below you will find a list of some of the foods that are the typical aphrodisiacs that are used today.

- Avocado: This fruit has been considered an aphrodisiac for a long time. The fruits high levels of vitamin E could be responsible for keeping the spark alive in the bedroom because it was meant to help maintain youth and energy.

- Bananas: Bromelain is an enzyme that is found in bananas and is known to trigger testosterone production. The spike in testosterone helps raise arousal in men.

- Chili Peppers: This bright red spice stimulates endorphins which can give you the same symptoms that you will feel when you are aroused.

- Chocolate: Dark chocolate can give you a chemical spike to make you feel pleasure, this is why chocolate covered fruit is a common choice of dessert foods for couples.

- Coffee: Caffeine is a stimulant that causes more blood to flow through the body. It is also highly thought of to put women into an aroused mood.

- Honey: Honey helps to maintain hormone levels while increasing energy.

- Olive Oil: The Greeks believed that olive oil made men more virile. It is also a great source of monosaturated and polyunsaturated fats which are needed to ensure that you are healthy.

- Oysters: This is probably the first thing people think of when they think of aphrodisiac foods. Oysters contain amino acids that aid in producing the hormones that are needed for sex.

- Pine Nuts: Zinc has been proven to be linked to having a healthy sex drive. Pine nuts are high in zinc, which is why they are considered an aphrodisiac.

- Pumpkin Seeds: These little seeds are incredibly high in magnesium. Magnesium helps to raise the levels of testosterone by ensuring more enters the blood stream.

- Strawberries: This fruit is great to feed to one another as a dessert that will keep the blood flowing to all regions of the body.

- Watermelon: This fruit is thought to have a Viagra like effect on the body because it relaxes blood vessels and as a result improves blood flow.

- Whipped Cream: While there is no scientific reason that whipped cream will boost libido, it can be incredibly erotic to eat with a partner and is sure to put it you in the mood.

There are many other foods that are considered aphrodisiacs, such as figs, cherries, pomegranates, artichokes, arugula and chai tea. With there being so many options you are sure to be able to put together a light meal or snack for you and your partner to enjoy together.

While it is believed that aphrodisiacs are going to actually increase sexual desire, they have been shared across all races and cultures. In essence, an aphrodisiac is the human's way of wanting to find a way for better sex.

Sadly, the FDA has found that there is actually no approach that is no medical that is going to work in increasing someone's sexual desire. But, that does not stop people from believing that an aphrodisiac will work.

Foods are one of the most commonly found aphrodisiacs in the world because they so closely resemble a person's genitalia. As mentioned above, there are a lot of different foods that are considered to be aphrodisiacs. Clams and oysters are most commonly associated with aphrodisiacs because of the way that they are shaped and the texture that the present when they are eaten. But, the truth is that they are going to be high in zinc which is something that many people lack in their diet and eating them causes a person to be more healthy therefore increasing their sex drive.

Spicy foods have given some scientific truth to the fact that food can increase one's sex drive. However, this is because of a spice that is found in cayenne pepper known as capsaicin that causes an increase in heart rate as well as metabolism. There may even be some sweating all of which are going to be similar to symptoms one might experience while they are having sex.

As strange as it sounds, okra is a vegetable that is rich in magnesium but is also a natural relaxant. All of the vitamins that are found in okra are good for your sex organs which can assist in increasing your sex drive. However, eating okra is not going to increase your sex drive just because you have ingested it.

Herbs are not often thought of as food, but they are used to spice food so they are still going into your body. One of the herbs that is most commonly associated with love is ginseng and that is because it resembles a human body. Plus, if you look at the translation of the name, it actually means man root. When ginseng was given to animals, there was an increase in sexual response, but sadly not in humans.

One herb that can be found in India as well as Africa is the Yohimbe which is thought to have the qualities of an aphrodisiac. It is thought that the Yohimbe wll stimulate the nerves that are located in the spine which can cause an erection without the need to increase sexual excitement. This herb is now known as the herbal form of Viagra.

However, if you are going to use this herb, you need to know that there are side effects that can be pretty severe. These side effects are overstimulation, hallucinations, anxiety, weakness, and even the possibility of paralysis.

I do not know about you, but I think I will stick to natural ways instead of risking those effects.

There are plenty of other aphrodisiacs out there that you can use, but as it has been mentioned, science has not actually proven that using these methods is going to increase your sexual desire. But, it never hurts to try does it? Even though you may try aphrodisiacs, you need to be careful about what some of the side effects could be. Not all of them are going to be severe and permanently harm you. However, an allergic reaction can slow down the desire pretty fast if you do ask me!

No matter what you do, enjoy your love making and have fun getting there!

Chapter 6: The Importance Of Communication During Lovemaking

The Kama Sutra places a large amount of emphasis on the importance of communication during the love making process. The ancient text discusses the many different ways that couples have to communicate with one another as they explore each other's bodies in sensuous ways.

The different types of foreplay that we have discussed throughout this book are all great ways for couples to begin communicating to stimulate lovemaking.

It is important to ensure that both you and your partner are comfortable with keeping an open communication throughout the entire process of foreplay and lovemaking. Failing to ensure that you are both communicating can result in one of the partners being unhappy with the experience.

Having open communication is even more important than you and your partner have made the decision to try something new. Ensuring that you are both getting enjoyment out of what you are doing is important. If your partner is not enjoying what you are doing, showing them that you respect them enough to stop and try something different is a great way to build trust in the relationship.

The Kama Sutra says that sexual intercourse is about communication and pleasure. If a lack of communication is preventing you or your partner from having their needs met, it can lead to unnecessary tension and unhappiness between the couple.

There are some things that you do and do not want to talk about when you are making love. When you communicate with your partner physically as well as verbally, you will discover that you are going to have more pleasure.

1. Allow your hands to do the talking. Not all communication has to be verbal and sometimes the nonverbal communication is more powerful. Try and add in both verbal and nonverbal cues when you are making love with your partner. For example, you should have your partner draw circles around your palm with their finger. As they do this, tell them things that you like such as the pressure they are applying; but, also tell them one thing they should change like the direction they are going.

2. Do not ask your partner if they have come yet! When your partner comes, it is going to be quite obvious to you! When you ask about it, you are going to make your partner find that it is hard to reach their climax. If they are in the middle of it and you do not know if they are orgasming or not, then you are going to end up getting them to stop orgasming. If you do not know if your partner is reaching their end, ask your partner to give you some kind of signal when they are so that you know that you have successfully pushed them over the edge.

3. Show that you like what your partner is doing! Moan, squirm, scream if you can! Let your partner know that they have found something that you highly approve of and want it to happen more.

4. Do not say things like ew or gross. When you do not like something that your partner is doing, try and use more positive statements rather than yelling and ruining the mood. So, if your partner's tongue goes somewhere that you think is gross, try and tell them something else that you would like over what they are doing. Do not be too critical with your statements or you are going to end the mood before you are ready for it to. Not only that, but you are going to make your partner feel bad and then they may be less likely to have sexy time with you again anytime soon.

5. Experiment with dirty talk. Sometimes it can be frightening to use dirty talk because you are scared of sounding like an idiot or going too far with it. While this is a common fear, do not let it hold you back. If you or your partner goes too far with the dirty talk, then tell them about it. Quiet sex is not always a bad thing, but noise can make it to where your partner knows what you like.

6. Do not check your phone! Phones are part of everyday life. But, this does not mean that you have to get on it right after sex. Spend a little time with your partner so that they do not feel like it was just business. Only check your phone if you absolutely have to.

7. You have the power to say no. if you are not comfortable with what is going on, then you should not stay silent. Let your partner know right away. And, never feel like you are doing something wrong when you say no. You are doing the right thing and protecting yourself.

Chapter 7: The Embraces Of The Kama Sutra

Now that you have set the mood in your pleasure room, and you are well versed on what foods are most likely to increase arousal in you and your partner, you are ready to begin exploring the many different aspects of foreplay. In this chapter, we are going to have a look at the types of embraces the Kama Sutra lists.

When it comes to the art of love, embraces are very powerful. The embraces we are going to be listing here are not your everyday hug. The Kama Sutra identifies twelve embraces that typically occur naturally in relationships, but can also be used as foreplay.

The Embrace Of The Breasts – This embrace is going to be when the male presses his chest between the breasts of his woman This is the type of embrace that would take place later during foreplay.

The Embrace Of The Forehead – This is another incredibly personal embrace. It is the gesture of affection and makes two partners feel connected. This embrace occurs when one party touches three different parts of their body to the same parts on their lover.

The Embrace Of The Jaghana – This embrace includes some pain which is not for everyone. Some people find that this little bit of pain adds to their experience. This embrace occurs when a man presses the area known as the Jaghana on his lover. This area is found between a woman's thighs and her naval with his own body as he gets on top of her. after this has happened, the pain will be applied through the use of teeth or nails.

The Embrace Of the Thighs – This embrace occurs when one of the two partners forcibly presses one or both of their partner's thighs between their own.

The Milk And Water Embrace – This embrace is often interpreted as making love with your clothes on. It is when a woman and a man will hold each other like they were trying to merge their bodies together and become one.

The Piercing Embrace – This embrace occurs when a woman bends down as if to pick something up and "pierces" a man with her breasts. The man would then take hold of them.

The Pressing Embrace – This is when the male presses his partner's body forcibly against a wall. Pairing this embrace with a deep kiss is a sure way to get both partner's blood flowing fast.

The Rubbing Embrace – This embrace happens when two lovers are walking slowly together and rub their bodies against one another.

The Sesamum Seed And Rice Embrace – This embrace happens when two people are on a bed together and they are going to be tangled together so that it is hard to tell where one person ends and the other begins.

The Touching Embrace – This isn't so much an embrace as it is a soft touch from one partner to the other. This embrace is when one partner subtly touches his partner with his body as he goes in front of or alongside her.

The Tree Climbing Embrace – This embrace is when a woman places one foot to that of her man and the other to his thigh. After this has happened, she is then going to lock her arms behind his back and all while sounding like a bird.

The Twining Of A Creeper – This is when a female clings to her lover in a way similar to how a creeper wraps itself around a tree. She uses both her arms and her legs and lowers his face towards as if her lips are going to be placed on his. This is an embrace that would only happen in private.

The act of embracing is an important way for foreplay to begin. There are four different stages to embracing. For couples who are previously unknown to one another, embracing is a great way to remove the distance between them, whereas a couple who is familiar with one another may approach embracing with a drive.

The four different methods to embracing are listed next.

Touching – The partners begin to touch one another while they are talking.

Pulling – The distance between the partners is closed by pulling each other close.

Rubbing – The partners begin to caress and stroke one another.

Pressing Hard – The partner's press firmly against one another in anticipation for intercourse.

As well as embracing, massage is another important type of foreplay. Massage has the ability to make your partner feel cherished and relaxed; these feelings will lead to a greater enjoyment when the actual act of intercourse takes place.

Giving a massage is not a difficult thing to do, and there isn't really a right or wrong way to do it, as long as your partner is enjoying it. Here are some tips to help make your massage successful.

- Use a massage oil or lotion that is scenting in a smell that you and your partner both find appealing. While a massage oil is not necessary, a nice oil will make the massage even more sensual than not using one.

- Begin your massage at the top of your partner's body, at the head/neck area. Run your hands from the neck, just below the hairline, down to the shoulder area.

- Use long strokes going down your partner's back ending right above their butt.

- Keep your strokes firm, but not hard. This is intended to be a sensual massage, as opposed to a deep tissue massage.

- Using different amounts of pressure, alternate between long soothing strokes, and circular motions.

- Massage the arms, using long sweeping strokes from the shoulder to the end of the fingertips.

- Using the same technique as you used on the arms, massages the legs down to the feet.

Foreplay should never be rushed, every touch and caress are helping you and your partner learn more about one another and what you each like and dislike as well as what leads to your arousal.

Now that we have covered all of the embraces that are a part of the Kama Sutra, as well as how to use massage to your advantage, we are going to move on and cover the different types of kisses that are included in the Kama Sutra.

Chapter 8: The Kisses Of The Kama Sutra

When it comes to the aspect of kissing in the Kama Sutra, it is a very in depth topic. There are four different kinds of kissing as well as many different techniques.

The Types Of Kissing

There are four different types of kissing according to the Kama Sutra. Those four types include contracted, moderate, pressed, and soft. The type of kiss you are going to use is dependant on the part of the body you are kissing. We are going to cover each type of kiss, as well as when it should be used, below.

Contracted – You would use this type of kiss after you have crawled your nails across the skin of your partner. This type of kiss is firm and meant to distract your lover's skin from the feeling of your nail moving across.

Moderate – This is the type of kiss that is reserved for the cheeks, mouth, breasts, belly, and hips where there is an abundance of flesh, and you can sink your teeth in without causing any real pain. This is an urgent type of kiss that is forceful and lingers on the edge of causing pain.

Pressed – This type of kiss requires the use of the tongue to trace the curves of the body. It is a sensual kiss that is intended to make your partner quiver with desire.

Soft – This is the kind of kiss that is used where the limbs meet the body, as well as the breasts. The tongue is used to tease gently and is broken up with gentle nips of the teeth. This kiss is so gentle that it requires the focus of your partner to really feel it.

The Methods Of Kissing

As well as the four types of kissing, there are different methods of kissing that are laid out by the Kama Sutra. Kissing is easily one of the biggest aspects of foreplay, and the different techniques allow us to use our lips to communicate the depth of our desire to our partner.

The Clasping Kiss – This kiss occurs when a partner takes hold of his lover's lips between his own. One partner taking control over the other in this fashion can be extremely sensual.

Fighting Of The Tongue – When a woman performs The Clasping Kiss on her partner, and he responds bt thrusting his tongue into her mouth it is considered to be a battle of the tongues for control.

The Greatly Pressed Kiss – This kiss requires the giver to take her partner's lips between her fingers and touching her tongue to her lover's lips before she can fully kiss his lips.

The Kiss Of The Upper Lip – This is an intimate kiss that is performed when the male is going to focus on the female's upper lip as she is focusing on his lower lip. This kiss is meant to ignite passion within the couple.

The Kiss That Awakens – This is a kiss that is performed on a sleeping partner with the intention of waking them up. Typically this kiss would be given by someone who has returned home late at night.

The Kiss That Kindles Love – This is a kiss that happens when a person looks upon their lover with admeration and kisses various parts of their face to show their desire for their partner. While this kiss is not intended to wake the sleeping partner, it is thought that the sleeping partner will feel the desire of the awake partner in their dreams.

The Kiss That Turns Away – This is a kiss that is used during an argument of disagreement to draw a partner's attention away from what they are focused on. This kiss is forced upon one of the partner's in hopes of drawing their attention to the instigating partner instead of the issue at hand.

The Pressed Kiss – This kiss is a hard passionate kiss that is performed at the time that the lips of our lover are pressed to our lower lip. The force coupled with only kissing the lower lip leaves our partner wanting more.

The Stirring Kiss – This is a kiss that is performed by a woman in a warm and seductive manner. It is said that when done correctly this kiss can make a man who is not in the mood for sex become aroused.

The Throbbing Kiss – This kiss concentrates on kissing the lower lip of your partner and ignoring the upper lip. It is intended to make your partner want more.

The Touching Kiss – This kiss is used when lover's lips first touch. The giver gently caresses one the lips of her lover with the tip of her tongue and grasps the hand of her partner while keeping her eyes closed.

The Turned Kiss – This kiss takes place when the giver grabs his partners hand and gently turns her face towards him with his free hand, turning her into the kids. This is a kiss that we often see in movies and strikes us as romantic as the man is playing a role of sensitive and forceful.

Vatsyayana described the different ways of kissing and also warned that everyone responds to different kisses differently, which plays an important role in a relationship. Since kissing is the first step towards a sexually active relationship, it is essential that it is enjoyed by both partners. If it is not something that is enjoyed by both partners, it can cause an abrupt halt to the relationship. Due to the important of kissing in foreplay, it is essential that you pay attention to your partner's cues to help you determine what they do and do not like when it comes to kissing methods.

Chapter 9: Pressing, Marking, Scratching And Biting

Embracing and kissing aren't the only aspects of foreplay that the Kama Sutra covers. It also places emphasis on using your nails and teeth to bring pleasure to your partner.

Nails

Using your fingernails to press, mark and scratch your partner when the action is becoming intense is only acceptable in four different situations. Those four situations are:

- The first sexual interaction with a partner;

- When one partner is setting out on a journey;

- When one partner returns from a journey; and

- After the reconciliation of a fight.

It is important to make sure that your nails are clean and free of any sharp edges before you engage in the act of pressing, marking or scratching your partner.

While the list in the Kama Sutra is not all encompassing of all the different types of marks you can leave on your partner with your fingernails, the Kama Sutra covers eight different types of marks.

Circle – This is two half-moons that are impressed opposite of one another, typically on the navel, buttocks, or the joint of the thigh.

Half Moon – This mark is typically left on the neck or breasts and is in a curved shape.

Jump Of A Hare – This this symbol cis going to be placed near the nipple and is five marks all near one another.

Leaf Of A Blue Lotus – This mark is in the form of a leaf and is made of the breast or the hip.

Line – This mark is is a simple line that can be located anywhere the person wishes it to be.

Peacock's Foot – this is a mark made on the breast by all five nails. The mark has a curved appearance and takes a high level of skill to do correctly.

Sounding – This is when the nail is pressed hard enough on the partner's skin to make a sound, but this is done with no pain and thus no mark is going to be left as evidence on the body. This is typically done on the chin, breasts, lower lip, and jaghana.

Tiger's Claw – This mark is usually left on the breast and is in the shape of a curved line.
In the situation where one partner is leaving on a journey, it is common to make a mark on the thighs or breast of their lover as a token of remembrance. This mark is comprised of three or four lines all close to one another.

Teeth

Another form of sexual communication is through the act of biting. The Kama Sutra explained that biting fuels the heat of love and said that all kissing points, other then the eyes, upper lip, and tongue are suitable for biting as long as your partner is willing. While a whole chapter in the Kama Sutra is devoted to covering the act of biting, Vatsyayana cautioned against using the teeth to hurt your partner. Below we are going to cover some of the more common types of bites. Notice that none of the bites break the skin, although some so leave marks.

Hidden Bite – This bite is typically done by the man. It is traceable bu the red mark it leaves behind, but there are no other markings. It is usually done on the lower lip of the receiving individual.

Swollen Bite – In order to execute the swollen bite, the biting partner must press down on either side of the place they are going to bite. This causes the area that is going to be bitten to swell upwards. This is typically done to the lower lip of the receiving individual.

The Biting Of The Boar – This is a bunch of bites that are done around the shoulders in proximity to one another. These bites are only deep enough to leave impressions and redness and are meant to appear as if an animal has been feasting.

The Broken Cloud – This bite is done by a man on a woman and involves the man biting areas on the woman's breast leaving uneven marks that look like a cloud that has broken up.

The Coral And The Jewel – This bite is meant to be done on the throat, thighs and thighbones for maximum pleasure. It is when a bite is done with all of the teeth as well as the lips. The biter brings their teeth and their lips together during the bite, with the lips being thought of at the coral and the teeth being the jewel.

The Line Of Points – This is a technique where the biter bites multiple times, hard enough to leave a mark. The marks make a line. No skin in broken in this technique, only red marks are left behind. This is usually done on the thigh, armpit or neck.

The Point – This is usually done on the lower lip. The biter uses only their two front teeth leaving two red spots.
Biting should never be done with the intention of breaking the skin, and is meant to ignite a heightened desire between two partners. It is important to ensure that you have your partner's consent before engaging in any marking, whether it is from the teeth or the nails.

The central agenda of the Kama Sutra is to turn sexuality into eroticism, but Vatsyayana did point out that unchecked ferocity of desire can overwhelm the erotic pleasure and lead to a loss of humanity. Because of this, he stated that both parties should be on the same wave of sexual energy in order to avoid one of the partners from coming off as being too aggressive.

Chapter 10: Striking – Where To Strike, How To Strike And The Noises Made

Vatsyayana compared intercourse to having a quarrel. The reasons for this included in the parameters is because of those who tend to argue with it.. The Kama Sutra was very specific with how it approached the act of striking. There are places that are considered appropriate to hit, specific ways to hold the hand while hitting and even different sounds that are acceptable from the recipient of the hits.

Since some people find the act of striking during foreplay to be incredibly erotic, while others find it to be a turn-off, this is another time it is important to ensure you are communicating with your partner.

Striking is intending to come as a surprise and a shock to the person who is being hit. Since it is coming as a surprise, it stands to reason that the person being hit is going to cry out. There are eight different kinds of noises that were listed in the Kama Sutra as being appropriate to make.

- The sound Hin. This is a long sound that is similar to "in" but without the "n" sound at the end.

- A loud booming noise referred to as a thundering sound.

- A sound of enjoyment, similar to a kitten that is mewling or a cooing noise.

- A weeping sound that is similar to crying.

- The sound Phut, similar to the sound you hear when something is dropped in the water.

- The sound Phat, similar to the sound heard when bamboo is being split.

- The sound Plat, similar to the sound phat, but louder.

- The sound Sut, this is a sound made with the tongue clicking on the teeth.

There were other words and sounds that were listed in the Kama Sutra, though not in as much detail. Some of the words had a specific definitions like the words "mother" and "father", which are words forbiddance. There are also other words that are these sounds are going to be sounds of freedom as well as of the pain that one is feeling along with praise for what their partner is doing to them. There are also sounds that belong to animals that are occasionally made use of. The animals that are used include various forms of birds such as a parrot or sparrow.

As well as having specific noises that could be made, there were also specific places that were appropriate to hit:

- The shoulders;

- The head, but not the face;

- The space between the breast, but not the breast itself;

- The back,

- The jaghana, or middle part of the body; and

- The sides.

There were also four specific ways that were considered to be appropriate to hold the hand if you chose to strike your partner.

Striking With The Back Of The Hand – These hits are meant to be aimed at space between the breasts during the act of intercourse. This space should be hit will increase up until Congress has come to an end.

Striking With The Fingers Contracted – This hit is meant to be made by the man to the woman's head while he makes the sound Phat. The woman should reply with the cooing sound and the sound Phut.

Striking With The Fist – These hits are meant to be aimed at the back of the woman when she is sitting on the lap of the man. She should return these blows to the man, abusing him as if she were angry at him.

Striking With The Open Palm Of The Hand – These hits can be aimed at any of the appropriate parts of the body, but they aren't meant to cause physical pain to the recipient, rather they are intended to increase the physical pleasure the recipient is feeling.

Lovemaking and sex are an activity that we all participate in at some point or another. Being on the same page as your partner regarding what you both enjoy as well as what you both consider being appropriate is an important aspect of learning what you are both going to enjoy. Striking can be something that adds depth to your lovemaking experience, as long as it is done correctly.

Chapter 11: The Basic Sex Positions

The Kama Sutra covered many different sex positions in addition to all of the aspects of foreplay we have already covered. Since the sex positions aren't the primary emphasis of the Kama Sutra, we aren't going to go too in-depth about the positions and instead, we are just going to cover some of the basic positions.

The Clasping Position – This is a position that happens when both the male and the female stretch their legs out over one another during intercourse.

The Erotic V Position – This position requires some flexibility and is accomplished when the woman is sitting on the edge of a table, and the man stands in front of her. The man may be required to bend his legs to bring himself to the height of the woman.

The Pressing Position – This begins as the Clasping Position that we saw above, and becomes the Pressing Position when intercourse begins, and the woman presses into her lover with her thighs.

The Rising Position - This position is achieved when the woman raises both of her thighs straight up in order to make herself more accessible for penetration.

The Splitting Bamboo Position – This position is when a woman places one leg over her lover's shoulder and then alternates which leg is up on the shoulder.

The Yawning Position – This position takes place when a woman raises her thighs and keeps them apart during intercourse.

Sammukha: the female is going to lean back against a wall with her legs spread. The male will then enter her. If you are a shorter female, you may discover that standing on something will make this position a little easier. Because of the contact, this position is very intimate and even offers for deeper penetration.

Janukurpara: you will need to be strong to do this position, so before you do it, you may find that you want to go to the gym some and get used to lifting some weight. As the male, you will lift up your female and lock your elbows just under her knees. Your hands are going to be on her butt and she is going to wrap her arms around your neck to help with the support.

Piditaka: you do not have to include acrobats in your sex life to make it thrilling. With this position, you are going to have your female lay on her back and bring her knees up to her chest. You are going to kneel in front of her and spread her thighs while giving her a little extra support by placing her hips on your thighs. From this position your female is going to feel as if she is tighter than normal being that her vagina is going to be more narrowed thanks to her legs being up. If you want to increase the pressure, have her cross her ankles or even bring her legs together more.

Virsha: in essence, this is just the reverse cowgirl. Just like the position is done with that name, you are going to have the female on top and she is going to impale herself upon his manhood with her back to him. She needs to be strong enough to hold herself up while you are flat on your back. While she rides you, you should enjoy the view!

Tripadam: if you are looking for a good position for a quicky, you are going to want to use this postion. You will both be standing and facing each other. She is going to bring one knee up to your hip and you are going to grab her leg just beneath her knee. Form here you are going to enter her and enjoy your fun!

Rocking horse: with the male sitting cross legged somewhere, he is going to support himself with his hands while the female sits on his lap and grinds her pelvis into his until he is inside of her. Once he is inside of her, the female is going to be able to rock back and forth until both of you orgasm.

Glowing triangle: first you will start out in the missionary position. After you have penetrated her, the male will get up on all fours, bringing the female's butt with her and applying pressure to her feet. The male is going to stay still once more while the female rolls her hips and brings both of them over the edge.

Nirvana: the female is going to lay on her back and stretch her legs out while the male gets on top of her and keeps her thighs on the outside of hers while penetrating her. There is going to be a lot of friction between the two and the male is going to do all of the work.

Ballerina: this position is much like a spooning position and it is extremely intimate being that your partner will be cradling you the entire time. To perform this act, you will lay beside him and lift whichever leg is on top so that he can get his legs in between yours. Being that he is behind you, you can bring your leg back to rest on his as he enters you and makes love to you.

Curled angel: as the female, you will lay on your side and curl your knees up so that they are touching your breasts. The male will then get behind the female and penetrate her from behind. The male and female are going to be close thus making this a romantic position. In order to bring more friction between the two, she can press her knees together more so that it narrows her vagina more.

Double decker: having the male lay on his back, the female is going to ease him into her before turning so she is not facing him. Now resting on her elbows, the female will be half laying on her partner and rocking his world.

The seduction: have the female on her back and bring her knees in. The male will get on top and enter her vagina. After that, she will move back and forth in what appears to be circles. This position also makes it to where the clit can be stimulated as well as other sensitive parts of the male's body.

Crouching tiger: getting on all fours, the male is going to stand behind his female and enter her. keeping her knees together is going to increase the love making.

Of course, this is just a brief overview of some of the positions that are in the Kama Sutra. The Kama Sutra goes much further into depth regarding the positions that are available for you to try. While it is not all inclusive, it is a great starting point if you are looking for new positions for you and your partner to try.

You can be as creative as you would like to work towards creating a positive atmosphere when you are in bed with your partner. You can use the positions above as a guide to see how limitless you can truly be when it comes to the position you are in when you engage in intercourse.

Conclusion

Now that you have gone through this book, you should have a good idea of the origin of the Kama Sutra and what it was intended for. It was not intended to be just a guide to the positions you can use to engage in intercourse; it was a guide to how to learn what you find to be pleasurable in your life and your relationships.

In its entirety, the Kama Sutra can help you to understand and decipher your desires and beliefs while also introducing you to a culture that is historically known for their sexual beliefs and practices.

This book has covered many of the different aspects of foreplay as they are listed out in the Kama Sutra. You have been advised on the different types of embracing, hitting, biting, marking and embracing. All of these things can help bring you and your partner closer. As you build on the connection you have with your partner; you are going to find that you begin to experience more happiness in other aspects of your life as well.

I hope that reading this book has helped you to learn more about yourself and has inspired you to share the wealth of knowledge you have received with your partner and use that information to your advantage.